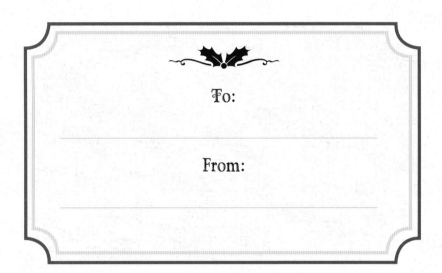

To:

From:

Text © 2012 Thomas S. Monson
Illustrations © 2012 Dan Burr
Art direction by Richard Erickson
Design by Sheryl Dickert Smith

Library of Congress Cataloging-in-Publication Data
Monson, Thomas S., 1927– author.
    The Christmas train / written by Thomas S. Monson; illustrated by Dan Burr.
        pages cm
    Includes bibliographical references.
    Summary: Thomas S. Monson, the President of The Church of Jesus Christ of Latter-day Saints, shares the story of the Christmas train from his childhood.
    ISBN 978–1–60907–182–0 (hardbound : alk. paper)
    1. Monson, Thomas S., 1927–   2. Gifts—Biography.   3. Christmas—Biography.   4. The Church of Jesus Christ of Latter-day Saints—Presidents—Biography.   5. Mormons—United States—Biography.   I. Burr, Dan, 1951– illustrator.   II. Title.
    BX8695.M56A3 2012
    289.3092—dc23
    [B]   2012017089

Printed in China
R. R. Donnelley, Shenzhen, Guangdong, China   10/13

10 9 8 7 6 5 4 3 2

THE
Christmas
Train

A True Story

THOMAS S. MONSON

Illustrated by DAN BURR

SHADOW
MOUNTAIN

I knew the question was coming, just like it came every year. My mother asked, "Tommy, have you thought about what you want for Christmas?"

I yearned as only a boy could yearn for a train. Not a common windup model train that was affordable; rather, I wanted one that operated through the miracle of electricity. I looked at my mother and replied, "I am hoping for an electric train."

The times were those when many families were not earning a lot of money; yet Mother and Dad, through some sacrifice, I am sure, presented to me on Christmas morning a beautiful electric train.

For hours I operated the transformer, watching the engine first pull its cars forward, then push them backward around the track. My new train went round and round with endless energy, and I never had to wind it up.

Mother entered the living room and said to me that she had purchased a windup train for Mrs. Hansen's son Mark, who lived down the street. Curious, I asked if I could see the train.

The engine was short and blocky, not long and sleek like the nicer model I had received. However, I did take notice of an oil tanker car that was part of his inexpensive set. My train had no such car, and I began to feel pangs of envy. I put up such a fuss that Mother surrendered to my pleadings and handed me the oil tanker car.

She said, "If you need it more than Mark, you take it."

I put the oil tanker with my train. Of course, my electric train with endless energy could easily pull the additional oil tanker car. I felt pleased with the result.

Soon afterward, Mother invited me to accompany her to the Hansen home. We gathered Mark's remaining cars and his windup engine and walked to his home down a nearby lane. I'll never forget the look on Mark's face when he received his train.

ark was a year or two older than I. He had never anticipated such a gift and was thrilled beyond words. He wound the key in his engine and was overjoyed as the engine and its cars, plus a caboose, went around the track.

Just before we were about to leave, my mother wisely asked, "What do you think of Mark's train, Tommy?"

When I looked up into her eyes, I felt a keen sense of guilt and became very much aware of my selfishness. I said to Mother, "Wait just a moment. I'll be right back!"

As swiftly as my legs could carry me, I ran to our home. I sprang up the porch steps and burst through our front door.

I picked up the oil tanker car, plus an additional car from my train set, flew down my porch steps, and ran back down the lane to the Hansen home.

I joyfully said to Mark, "We forgot to bring two cars that belong to your train." I don't know who was happier, Mark or my mother. What I do know is that was the day when I felt in my heart that giving had replaced getting.

Mark coupled the two extra cars to his set and placed them on his track. "Do you want to stay and watch with me?" he asked excitedly.

I looked back at my mother who, of course, nodded her approval. I couldn't help but smile and say, "Sure!"

I watched the windup engine make its labored way around the track and saw Mark's face beaming. I felt a supreme joy, difficult to describe and impossible to forget. The spirit of Christmas had filled my soul.

"Jesus said unto him, Thou shalt love the Lord thy God with all thy heart, and with all thy soul, and with all thy mind. This is the first and great commandment. And the second is like unto it, Thou shalt love thy neighbour as thyself."

MATTHEW 22:37–39